AF446455
Pockets
Of
Lavender
a poetry
collection
Kendall Hope

Advanced Praise for *Pockets of Lavender*

"Kendall has a never-ending romance with the earth and with humanity. The poems are childlike on one page and deeply sensual on the next, keeping me on my toes as I read. I thoroughly enjoyed the book!"
— Joey Doherty, Author of *Subtle Medicine*

"Kendall writes about embracing the moment; that every moment or state is perfect just as it is. An easy read and very insightful."
— Courtni A. Tansey, Author of *Ready To Evolve*

"Kendall has such a descriptive way with her words. Her illustrations and photographs add such a beautiful and personal touch, and I can genuinely say this book helped me enter the states of loving, being, and feeling. Perhaps one of my favorite poetry collections."
— Flor Ana, Author of *Nourish Your Temple*

"A truly wonderful and dreamy book of poetry. Kendall really knows how to capture the delicate beauty and essence of life itself."
— Jenna Nicole Stevens, Author of *Magic & Musings of the Universe*

"*Pockets of Lavender* is a treat for springtime and summertime hearts. Kendall Hope serves ripe poems for readers to bite into with a hint of hope, longing, exploration, and kindness."
— Cheyenne Raine, Author of *Maroon Daydreams*

"Breathtaking and awakening from the first page. *Pockets of Lavender* takes us on a journey through all of the emotions. Each poem is like putting a mirror up to your soul and feeling everything all at once."
— Vincent J. Hall II, Author of *The Drinks Between Us*

*Disclaimer: Reviews have been edited for length and clarity.

"I felt many emotions while reading *Pockets of Lavender*. Writing about nature, human experiences, and love is something that many people can connect to. Kendall wrote in such a beautiful way and was able to bring her poetry to life with vivid imagery. Truly a beautiful piece of work."
— Emma Gilman, Author *of Walking A Tightrope*

"Beautiful. That is the word that describes the poetry in this book. Each poem is crafted to make the reader feel what it means to have complete awareness of the life around you. Kendall Hope's poetry is like the most perfect bouquet of flowers; every time you look at it, you smile and a waterfall of bliss falls down on you."
— Amelie Bauer, (Starred Review)

"There is a particular wonder that can be said about people who can make mundane things beautiful and complex things, not only within your understanding, but reveal their elegance entirely. This collection of poems encompasses a sort of odyssey through the mind of a young woman grappling with her own evolution and perspective of the world around her. Saying this is an amazing read doesn't do it enough justice."
— Michael Billig, (Starred Review)

*Disclaimer: Reviews have been edited for length and clarity.

Pockets of Lavender

a poetry collection

Kendall Hope

Indie Earth Publishing Inc.
| Miami, FL |

INDIE EARTH
PUBLISHING

Pockets of Lavender

To Jessy

"IF"

If I were a angle in heaven,

And you were a star in the sky,

I'd sit on the edge of a pink cloud

And smile, as my cloud floated by.

Then I'd go to the top of the rainbow

And slide down to the tip of your star,

And there I would hang my halo

Way up in the heavens so far.

And if you should sprinkle some stardust

On my wings, and I'd ask you why,

Maybe you'd say you were lonely,

Almost as lonely as I.

And then if the earth should light up
With a glow from way up above,
They'd know that a star and an angle
Were happily falling in love.

Carol

Foreword
by Flor Ana

Edgar Allan Poe once said, "Poetry is the rhythmical creation of beauty in words."

Poetry has always had a special place in my heart. From the time I first learned to read to the way I manage to compose my thoughts and clear my mind, and the writing of my own poetry books. As I've grown older, dove deeper into this literary world, I'm so blessed to say I have discovered such a beautiful community of poets, and among all those talented hearts, I'm so grateful to not only call Kendall Hope a mentee, but a friend.

I met Kendall before she began her journey into writing *Pockets of Lavender.* She had asked me to be her mentor in the poetry publishing process. I had never been a mentor, but something in my heart and soul told me to do it, to connect with someone two thousand miles away and help them achieve a dream that I, myself, still dreamt.

Together, Kendall and I took the plunge to create the book you have now in your hands. This is Kendall, all of her, and I'm so glad to have been a part of this experience, to let my petals bloom in the same soil hers does. Sometimes, that's all you need to push you further in your adventures, your journey; someone to be there with you along for the ride.

What began as weekly Zoom calls to go over poems became a beautiful, blossoming friendship, and for that, I have no words. Every time Kendall would show me a new poem for this collection, my heart would flutter. Her words are absolutely beautiful and descriptive, and before we had even discussed the book sections, her words were making me feel, be, and love. Then, her illustrations and photographs further made the words on the pages come alive. It was beautiful to witness her growth from aspiring writer to author in the time we worked together. Those eight months seemed to have flown by.

This book has become a favorite from start to finish, and I hope you see in it the value that I do. I'm looking forward to what else Kendall will bring to the poetry and literary communities and how this book will touch hearts around the world.

May you see Kendall's beautiful soul through her inspiring words and find comfort and ease in these pockets of lavender.

Table of Contents

Table of Contents

Table of Contents

Pockets
(State of Feeling)

The Yellow Kitchen

Sitting next to the sun room,
playing our own card games
While we set the placemats and newspapers
onto the stools, out of our way
Hearing your cackled laugh

And remembering some years ago
Sitting at those stools
As you pretended to wait on us
and shuffled your feet along the floor,
giving us our princess cups
And I remember reading aloud,
out of *Nat Geo* magazines
Making up facts
that you went along with

To the days I got older
And held your hand
And outgrew the height of the hearth,
that we used to reach for
And playing the slot machine downstairs
with a tin bucket full of nickels
Maybe while a puzzle sat on the table unfinished,
between a kind old man & a glimmering young lady
With a scent of *M&Ms* and cigarettes present

Feeling all those years of memories
On that yellow kitchen wall
Where we kept growing tall

Effervescent

Let that personality of yours never fizzle out
Stay bubbly about the things you love,
for what you attract sparkles like cider
Sweet and rosy, you blush like strawberry wine
Your lips are tinted like a cherry,
as you grin with squinty eyes

Bathe

Let your skin soak and your worries evaporate
Feel anchored, but not sinking
Keep your head above water and breathe
Sense the warm steam around you
The essence of candlelight, soap, and scents releases and eases
Think and feel
And rinse off your energy for the night

Newborn

That exciting new baby you once were
You had no real personality or thoughts yet
Then you grow, and change, and make mistakes
And you turn into this lovely big human
But it is old news
So make life exciting for yourself
Because you are still that little baby that came from this universe
And it is still within you
Let us adore these new children
Truly let them learn and feel loved and exist
For they will be adults one day
And their happiness should always stay

Captive

Stop trying
To give your wings
To those who
Hold you captive and cocooned

Little One

Lady bug, lady bug fly away home
but do not forget to let your mind roam
Those wandering thoughts are okay to explore
because some feelings we can not ignore

Grasshopper, grasshopper where did you go
and how can you travel to me to and fro
You hop season to season with loose or tight grasp
and oh I know those ever changing emotions,
should never be masked

Little snail, little snail I will follow your trail
and know you will allow me to wail when I feel frail
Though you may have slow progress in each new day
let us not underestimate the pace you may stay

The Wave of a See You Next Time

Of lover and family
On Blue Gill & Friendship Lane West
Both so pleasant
I see you all in one another
As you stand
And I see your silhouettes
In the doorway and the front lawn,
under the porch light
A wave for next time
And I admire you all,
for you are my favorite beings
And I honk goodbye for now
For there is always a next time
Whether it is after some kisses,
a game of *Scrabble*,
or some hours of talking.

Crash & Burn

Am I really like a Phoenix?
How many times must I have to emotionally fall repeatedly,
Before I rise again
Each time.
How many times must the world pluck my feathers
Before I keep my fiery grace?
Knowing its always there in me,
When will they stop turning me to ashes,
Though I assume the cycle is inevitable
And I rise & survive,
Each time.

Green

That color green
more of a sage
Exploding in my eyelids
as they close
and I feel close to you
A rare phenomenon
but oh so lovely to see
and to feel
That color green

Snowfall

Lay in the snow
And feel the tickle on your cheeks
as you look up
And the little specks fall into your eyes
Shake hands with the pine
and let the falling snow hiss
Barely a whisper
as it hits the ground
And now you must go inside
though you may not want to
For your toes will soon blister
from the cold's magic numbing
Watch & listen
as the world is only a buzz
Gaze at this powder
that looks like cotton fuzz

Rolling Words

My muscles quiver
And my skin shutters
As your voice rolls down my back
In the dark of night

Deja Vu

The way the deja vu flows through my eyes
into the reality of my days
I have seen this before
I have felt this before

That familiar feeling
of my life being aligned
Do those wishes on eyelashes and dandelions
make a difference in my timeline
I shall blow on them anyways
no matter the events meant to happen

Life takes me along its current
and sometimes gives me glimpses of the future in my dreams
Though I forget them in the morning

But when the deja vu flows through my eyes
into the reality of my days
I know life has its fateful events laid out over me like a blanket
So I shall live and I shall see
what life thinks is meant for me

The anger

There is no point in furthering anger,
but to build a bigger gape in one's soul
To tiptoe around the frustration of others,
but still not knowing the right steps or goal
Even if nothing you try works,
and they grow malicious and cruel
Just know that kindness prevails,
for coal being burned, creates a jewel
The darkness may strike that golden heart of yours,
but don't let it overgrow and root
Anger should never be a chore

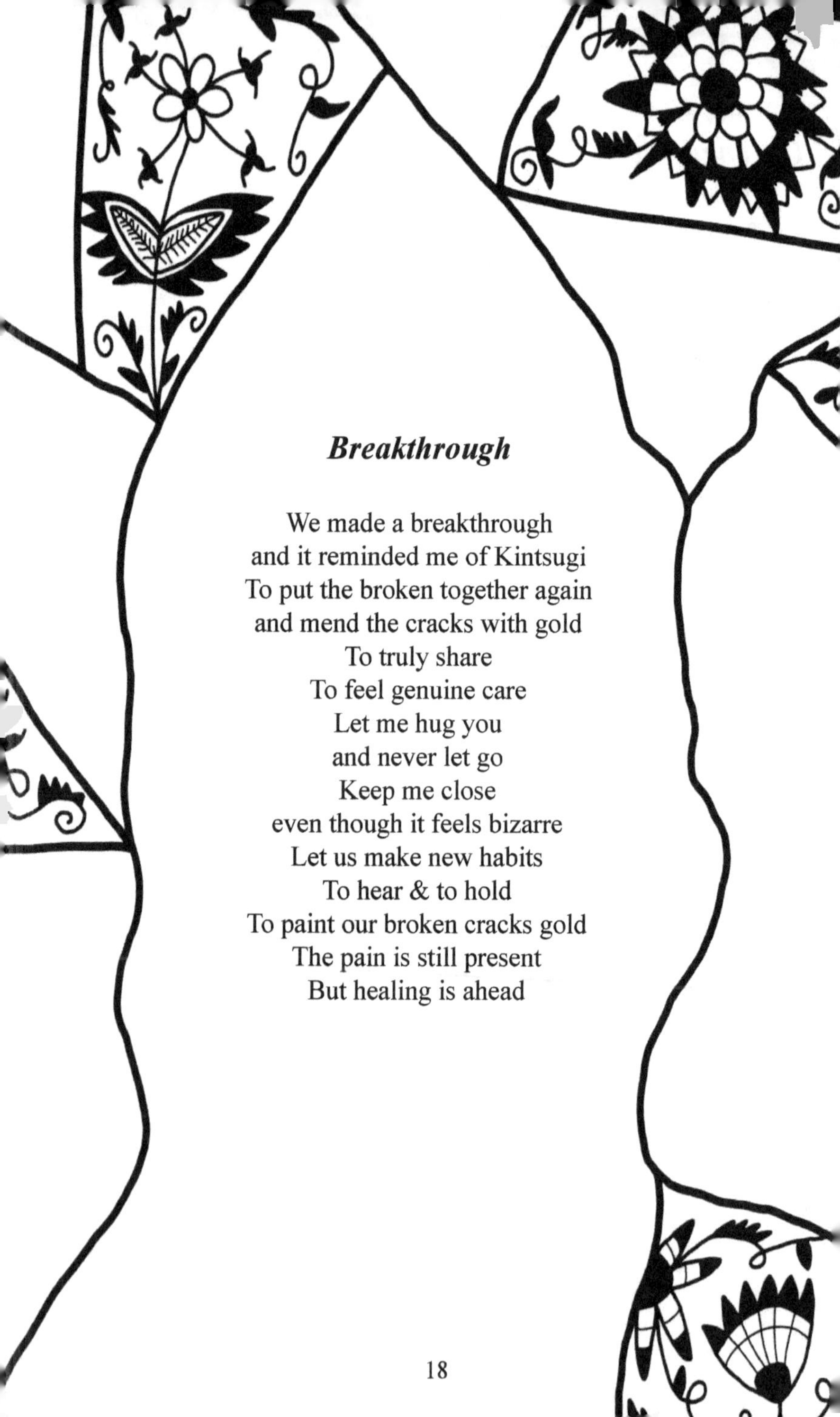

Breakthrough

We made a breakthrough
and it reminded me of Kintsugi
To put the broken together again
and mend the cracks with gold
To truly share
To feel genuine care
Let me hug you
and never let go
Keep me close
even though it feels bizarre
Let us make new habits
To hear & to hold
To paint our broken cracks gold
The pain is still present
But healing is ahead

Spill

I wish you could hug my soul
to squeeze the emptiness
and let the tears puddle out
I feel a whole lot, while feeling nothing at all
The emotions collide and cancel out
spilling through my eyes,
for they are the window to my soul's current state
Feel the slow rhythm of my heart spread,
while my brain whispers loud thoughts to yours
I know it is okay to feel this one out,
but maybe your existence alongside mine,
could help soothe my aching body
So fill me with warmth from your patience of my essence
While I am trying my finest

Medusa

With my long, curly locks
Like *Medusa*, I am
I will turn you to stone
With my kind and fearsome eyes
For you've turned my heart stone first
And I find ways to keep growing

Twin size bed

Waking up in the morning
With that certain feeling
of warmth, softness, & relaxed muscles
between dream state & reality
In the twin size bed I have always had
Petting my dog
and feeling the weight of them on my legs
feeling perfectly comfy
A rare, but magnificent feeling

SEX

Kiss every beauty mark you find
Tracing my outline
The curve of my spine
My legs feeling long and stretched
among my hips & bones
Feel the pattern of our breaths
While I hold your hands tightly
Make sex exist beautifully & break the taboo
It is inevitable and indefinitely me and you
Such a burning passion
With my eternal flame

That funny feeling

That funny feeling
to love who you love
to admire person to person
All for who they are,
not what they are

Twin flames

To carry the flicker of a soul who is not lost,
but feels disconnected
Do not leave my grasp, darling,
for with every human experience this universe throws,
our souls together are twin flames,

A flame that flitters with anxiety,
is trailed by smoke that a slow depression follows

But when your soul feels limp
I will lift you with all my being
For our souls could be lighter than the gas of a fire,
but we are still eternal and can feel heavy emotions, my dear.

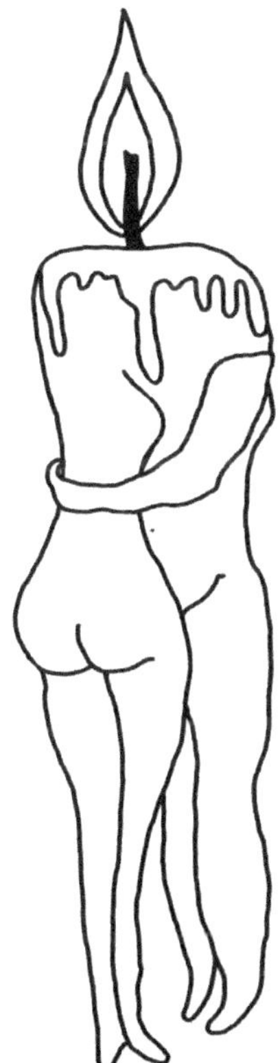

Of
(State of Being)

Artist's point of view

With a body like a cherub or the birth of Venus
Notice how the artist views existence
and everything becomes beautiful
Detailed and vulnerable
You are art
Society counts the insecurities
Stomachs, noses, folds
Unique is lovely
And even if you fit more modern beauty standards,
love the parts of yourself that society finds dismissive
Mind, body, soul
What do we turn into wherever we go
Be the art and exist in your form
We are human BEINGS after all

Golden Blue Hours

Nature's first green is gold,
Oh, so I am told
So I wake
And the morning takes
Me into the fresh forenoon
A caterpillar hidden away,
Glistens in its cocoon
And oh that blue hour
I notice after I step out of the shower
Must I admire
That beautiful fire
That night leads into day

Ghost

I saw a ghost
Made of skin and bones
I saw its past self and heard the ghost groan
There and gone in the blink of an eye
What were they here for, I wonder why

I saw a ghost
Yet I was not scared
For they lived here too and I could only stare
A friend visiting our reality, living the unknown
I felt the shiver of them, as the wind had blown

I saw a ghost
And realized they are always around
The past, present, and future, always surrounds
No need to fear, the death of memories or oneself
One day, you will be a ghost, perhaps visiting at night
on the hour of the twelfth

The abandoned home

That leaning tree among the broken shack,
The place I pass and have always wanted to photograph,
Every season I watch time pass,
Just off the highway, left untouched.

Fairytale

To relax in a bed of green
With a tulip overhead
A tiny firefly lighting the inside of its petals
I read amid the blades of grass
Watching the stars
Breathing in and out
A ladybug curled at my feet
I am a little fairy
With nothing to worry

Lady Lamp

The lady lamp
Found in an antique booth
along the Seaside
Catching my eye
Never leaving my mind
With that tulip shaped ceramic dome
that reminds me of the ones in my comfort home
She curves so delicately along the mirror she leans
Knowing you see her
for she is lovely
Among the flowered trim
you trace your fingers gently along her lifted arm
In space number 84
I hope to return
to take her away
And admire her eternal stance
Standing on the edge of the lamp
I would cherish her forever, but for now,
just her memory will do

NASIM (nah-seem)

They have such grace, power, and spirit,
Even when shoved down,
I will help lift you,
Just this one occurrence
Your name, meaning fresh air or breeze,
A butterfly floats past us,
And we breathe,
Smelling that pocket of lavender,
In such short time,
We breathe together,
And lavender's entity
Now entirely changed, ongoing,
Til I take my last breath,
Perhaps with the scent in my mind.

Fog

Fog on the drive home,
Engulfed,
Every one of my atoms condensed
And surrounded,
Headlights like ghost eyes glaring at me,
Not visible until inches away,
The fog & mist keep coming my way,
I am swallowed by a monster whole
Though I am not scared,
I feel a sense of calm,
No relativity to time,
The lights beam blurrily around me,
Like fireflies stuck in a whale's mouth,
I am one too.

Tree Rings

The rings of a tree
They tell a story
Of each year of its life
Each one telling how much rain had fallen
How much weeping there was for the willow
Big and small
Thick and thin
So much happens in a year's time
And guess what
The tree has survived each one
Up until this very moment,
So have you, my dear
Among every rainstorm and every year

The orange morning

The deep orange rays shine through the shutters
and melt along the edges of framed paintings
As the morning lies sleepily
waking with dew & a yawn
As the world awakes
and noise steadily chirps through the walls

Moon beams

You & the Moon beam
powerfully my lady,
Going through each of your phases
Sometimes like a cheshire cat's smile
She glows
Even when she does not feel luminant
She is still there

The Anatomy of a Woman

Her breasts, can be any shape or size
And they nourish her through confidence
and being a shield for her heart
And they nourish her children
if SHE decides to bear
Oh and do not forget
not to mind the body hair

Her ovaries, tiny yet mighty
That uterus makes her stomach have a little pouch
that sticks out, no matter her size
For it protects
the eggs that may flower
For no matter the pain they inflict on her body
She is *strong*
So *strong* she can feel the waves of pressure
that crash down inside her
As she cramps, as she swells

Though her breasts are visible
It's the invisibility of the uterus
that mustn't be overlooked
For within the cycles created for a woman
She prospers
Every day
Every week
Every month
Every year
Because being a woman comes with such grace
So look her in the face
And see her to be more than her lips & her thighs
See the sparkle of *strength* in her eyes

43

Napped

I watched the pale sunlight
Shine on his face as he napped
The sweet, mysterious shadows
Dancing on his fragile and tan skin

Waltz

I've taught you to skip in the sun
As you've taught me to waltz in the snow
Now let us bathe in the moonlight serenade

45

I've taught you to skip in the sun
As you've taught me to waltz in the snow
Now let us bathe in the moonlight serenade

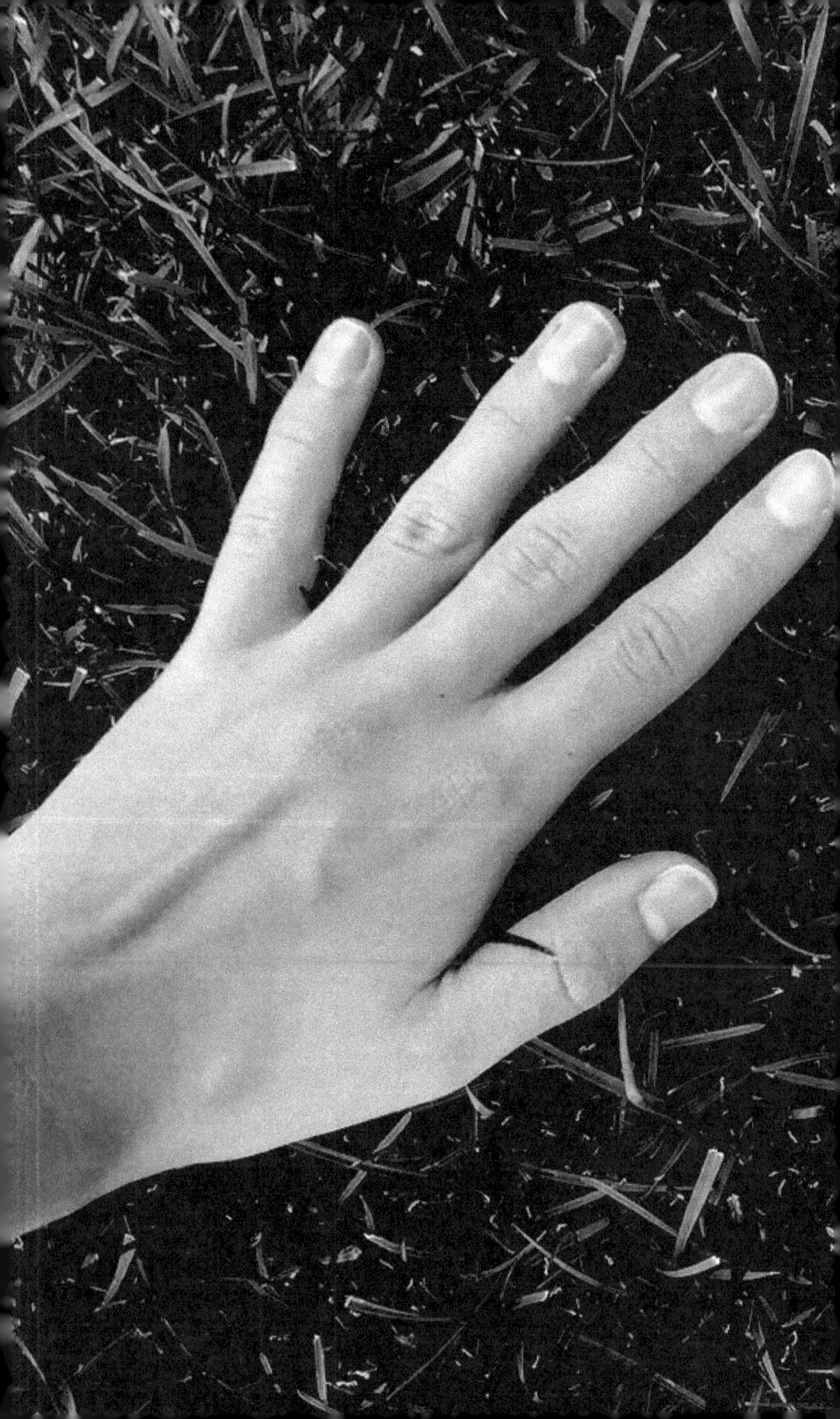

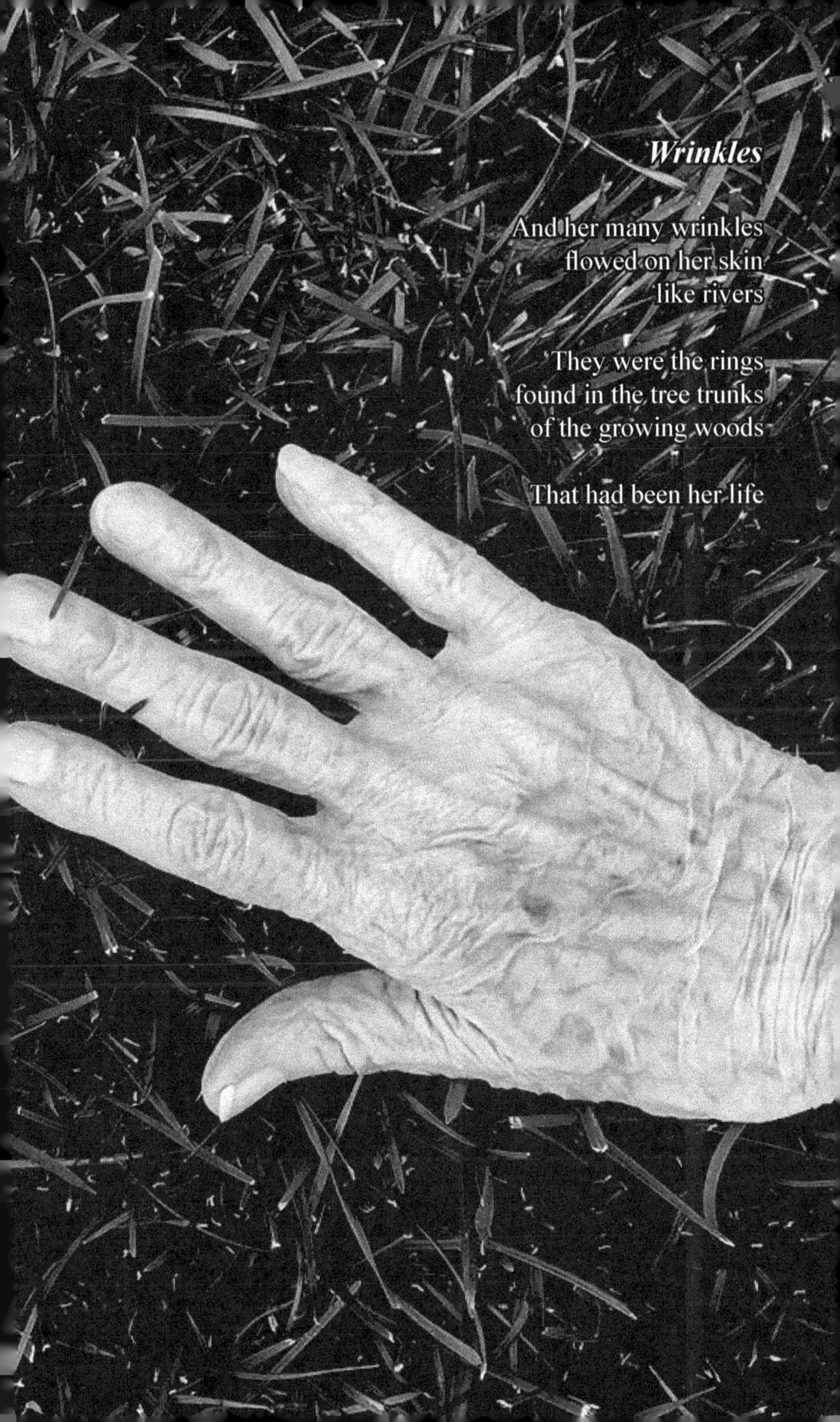

Wrinkles

And her many wrinkles
flowed on her skin
like rivers

They were the rings
found in the tree trunks
of the growing woods

That had been her life

Nonexistent

A humble, little bumble bee
Only making but 1½ teaspoons of honey in its life
Must we eat that golden syrup
Without a second thought
For that tiny, yellow, fuzzy-jacketed friend
Doesn't deserve an end
They do so much to make the world flourish
So to them, we must keep them nourished
If you find yourself stumbled upon a tired worker
Give them some sugar water
And if you are ever on a walk
And hear a quick buzz
Do not be frightened
Be enlightened
For this creature that often gets overlooked
Does much for this big ball of earth
For without their existence
We will cease as well

Snow Day

Have your snow day, my angel
Like a child missing school
Time to make toast
Put on warm socks
Make some cocoa
after playing in the piles of frost
Do not worry about time
Play and flow
in the piles of snow
Be a child my dear
This occasion really happens only once a year
Watch new or old movies
under the blankets
Play in the powder
with your puppies
Let them pounce and chase and get covered
with white freckles
Let your feet warm on the vent
Though you did not mind getting cold this time

The space around us

I am day & you are night
Somehow we fit together just right
In distance
We communicate like Earth to a satellite

I am yours & you are mine
Our thoughts and minds intertwine
You & I together, a beautiful sight
We dance in rhythm with the starlight

Never to run out of time
We sparkle like fine wine
Darling, it's always our time to shine.

When I Die

When I die,
Spread me along the grounds of the earth
Let the moss cross over my remains
Let the weeds of the forest floor devour and tangle
What once was my bones and flesh
Let the mushrooms be fed from the dust of my human form
Let the flowers bloom from where my heart once beat
Let the leaves descend on me and create a bed for my soul to rest
When I die,
Let me be where I belong
Among the earth from where I became

Humans

How sweet and simple we can be as humans
We dance and we wiggle to strange noises and beats
We jump into puddles we find on the streets
We have our own languages that make us stutter or flow
We blush red with awkward encounters that make our cheeks glow
We move our bodies clumsily or with grace
We smile at strangers, each a new face
We bellow odd noises when we have a laugh
We shiver and cuddle when there is a cold draft
We scrunch up our faces and squint to see
Oh if we could not have the joy of being human,
What would we be?

Lavender
(State of Loving)

Honey do, honey dew?

Honey, do you think of me,
with the fresh summer breeze?
At the farmers market do you
smell that sweet honey dew residue?
Honey, do you taste the juice of the honeysuckle when I miss you?
On the car ride home in my grocery tote,
do you wait to be devoured on the kitchen counter?
Honey dew, you feel fulfilled with each bite
taken out of you in the prime of your ripeness?
Honey do, honey dew,
Do you taste the hue of the honey's dew?

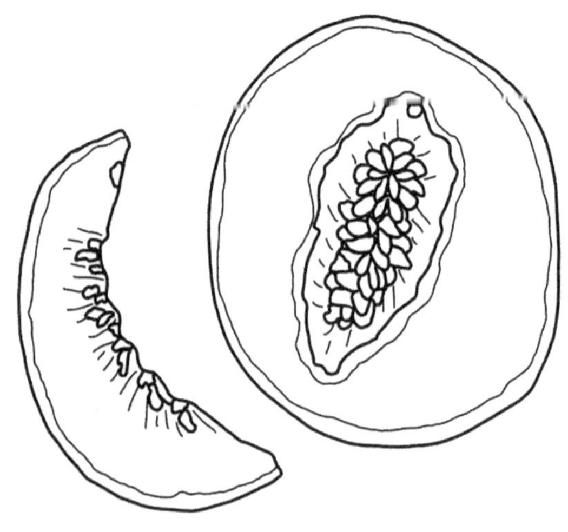

Forget me not

Forget me not, my darling
For like the fragile flower
I would turn blue
And wither away
Without my sunshine

Magical Body

Your body is magical
With its rolling shoulders
Those spots and bumps
you get on your skin
Those lines on the back of your legs
under your curves
Your stomach
when it is a little more round than usual
Your eyes when you smile
and one closes a little more than the other
Because,
You are breathing,
Your heart is pumping,
Your muscles are moving,
Your bones are protecting,
Your brain is thinking,
You are living.

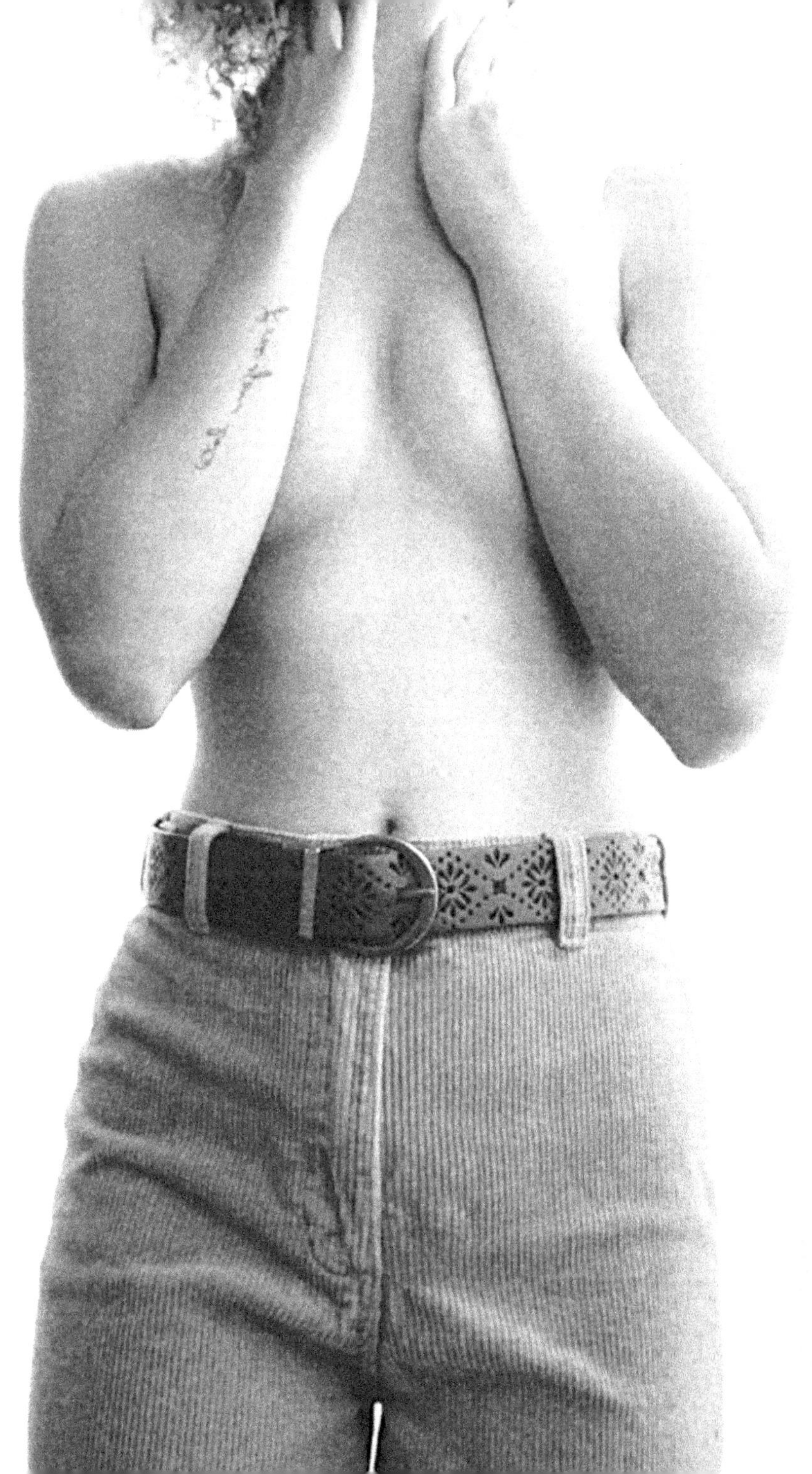

April & May

Kiss me gently
Amongst the fields of flowers
That the showers of April
Fell upon May

Flor

Flor, meaning flower
Oh, she has such great power
With never ending growth that travels far
She is as unique as the stars
Flor gives you an instant gratitude
Meeting her each Tuesday excites and rids you of attitude
She makes you feel heard when you are vulnerable
Flor will help you if you were to tumble
Flowers may seem delicate,
but they are colorful and sturdy
Just like Flor,
Who I will remember until I am one hundred and thirty

Skinny

You're so skinny, they say
they mean it as a compliment
But it has gotten old, & rather dreary
they are not the ones who live in my body
My temple, My home
My ribs are the rafters
keeping my frame
Steady & skinny
Oh it's so mundane
to hear how I am so thin

It's the way I've always been
and the way I'll probably always be
But the trick is you see,
I see myself for the flowers that bloom
even when my body feels gloom
Because I see the strength that my body holds
even when it feels cold

Kendall Hope

Peekaboo Moon

"Peekaboo!" says the moon.
Peeping through the morning's new blue,
greeting the sun for its early rising shift.

The sun beams a smile back and says,
"Sleep well, my tired friend!"
for the moon needed rest for its next shining night.

And so, mister moon prospers from lady sun's ultraviolet light.

Dancing old

Spin me around the room
As we transport
To the olden days
While you make me swoon
Full of giddiness and dancin'
Slow & close
While my hips sway
Gentle & endearing
In my flowy dresses
Until you spin them right off
Teleported through the music
And feeling that old love of two souls
Keeps us dancin'
Til our skin grows old
Feel the love in the room flicker
Like the candle light we spin in
Til the wick grows cold

Amelie

Oh sweet Amelie,
The girl who writes poems about you,
Keen and kind,
Let us watch you adventure,
Let us watch you grow,
You inspire,
With just a smile,
Unapologetically and remarkably yourself,
Keep using your words,
For you are so wise, resilient, and true,
Chase the sunshine,
For your warmth is endless,
Never fear, you've only yourself to bear,
May you always be,
Sweet Amelie.

I Love Myself

I love myself
For the variety of curls in my natural hair
For the tiny forest that I grow on my legs
that I wear with pride,
For their length & appearance,
that others can not seem to bear
For my unique nose
For my rolled shoulders
For my webbed toes
For my rounded cheeks
And my little scars
I love myself
For I am just as great & individual as the stars

Mother dearest

You are the rock
Through tumbles and cracks
you manage to grow flowers among those fractures
You take on the waves that run yourself smooth like limestone
yet your tough interior cannot wear down entirely
Believe me when I tell you
you are more beautiful than you feel
Your aura glows like a rose quartz
and is full of unconditional love
I can see the aches in your bones and soul
but mother dearest, you move mountains
You are our rock

My Cowboy

Let me daydream in your mountain home
where each year I have grown
Living in my happy place
where I make visits to see your face
A man who never seems to grow old
among many stories the years have told
Sitting on your porch with mountain's gold
Talks from morning to night
while you protect me now in this life
One day, but no time soon
say hello to me in my dreams
You are my old Cowboy who gleams

Seasons

Snow falls from the sky like powdered sugar on my plate
We sit, at breakfast, on a cold Winter date

We relax among blades of green
They itch my arms, though I do not mind
Spring with you is peachy keen

The sun kisses our skin
Leaving behind a blissful tint,
I still feel the warmth of you
Even after the Summer sun turns blue

I crunch the leaves as we walk through the orange abyss
Holding your hand & awaiting a kiss
I am reminded with memories of us from each of our autumns
A feeling of nostalgia and warm, sweet love
Covers me like a blanket

Kisses

He hopes his lips never become too weak to
kiss my own
He fears that one day his body will be too
frail to appreciate mine
Yet our souls will never grow weak
And I'll watch him twitch in his sleep
As he takes on the world
And beats himself up for not feeling
like he has done enough

So let me take the tangled mess that makes up
your thoughts, sweet boy
And untie all the knots
Let us take our time
For there is no rush
When I can count your freckles with my lips
And kiss under infinity

Honey & Wallpaper

Honey & Wallpaper
In that little, pleasant valley
On friendship lane,
Hands of wrinkled silk
Laced with my youthful fingers
And an aura like honey,
You radiate inside and around me,
The green floral wallpaper
I stare,
You say I remind you of your younger self
Even after you join the stars,
You can live furthermore through me,
Vicariously & evermore,
Until I return to the stars,
And hold your hands of silk,
Once again.

Feeling

I like the feeling
of your heart
Thumping through my bones
onto my back
and through my soul
As I hear your breath
tapping on your ribs
As our chests
rise and fall in sync
Like our heart beats
for one another
And to feel
The rumbling of your voice
and how it flows
Through my ears
To the parts of my brain
That you constantly occupy
When my head lies
on your chest

Seize

The patience and ease
He has as he holds you
While your hands seize
Unable to grasp him back
Your arms are stuck and feeling immobile
Your heart reaches
And he holds
And he holds
And he holds

Sisterly Warmth

Let her decide when she wants to be your friend
The fire of friendship is there nonetheless
through our blood
Whether the spark is among burned embers,
or a warm glow
As we learn to two step in the living room
or slam our doors
You are my sister, evermore

Sunday Kind of Love

Give me that Sunday kind of love
Where I can kiss you in the kitchen
Get tipsy & eat ice cream on the floor
Dance in each room as you hold my hips
And eat snacks in bed
You can brush my hair after a warm shower
And read in front of our sunny window
as the sun catchers glitter rainbows on the floor
And eat brunch on the small patio
Where we forget time exists
Do chores together
And visit the local market
We can watch movies that I will fall asleep to
while in your arms
I want that Sunday kind of love

27

To turn 27 on the 27th. It is your golden year, my dear. Though I hope you see, all the gold that has already been brought to your years. Looking back at these words on your golden birthday, what do you think and what do you feel? How many of your ambitions have become real? As you write this, you are only 20 years young. Have you chosen to stay kind, patient, and fun? I hope you have created and I hope you have loved. To always nurture your life, and be reminiscent of. I hope you've made and explored lots of adventures. And even gained some new favorite colors. You have gone through so many seasons now. Keep living more golden years that your heart allows.

If you would like to further support Kendall, please take a moment to leave reviews on Goodreads, Barnes & Noble, and Amazon.

Thank you.

"*Your thoughts deserve a decent place to live.*"

\- R. Clift

Music Artists

I love every single song each of these artists has ever made:

84

Still Woozy

Harry Styles

Jenny Lewis

Billie Eilish

Songs That Make Me FEEL Every Time:

May this playlist give you your own lovely feelings
and some more insight into my brain.

85

Pockets of Lavender:

Notes & Acknowledgments

"If" by Carol Foltz (Nanny)

"Little One" Photograph by Michael Billig

"Green" Photograph by Michael Billig

"Golden Blue Hours" was inspired by
Robert Frost's "Nothing Gold Can Stay"

"Tree Rings" Photograph ("Stumped") by Michael Billig

"When I Die" Photograph by Michael Billig

"I Love Myself" was inspired by
"I Like Myself" by Karen Beaumonth

Author Photo by Jamie Podoll (My Mother Dearest)

Notes & Acknowledgments

I cannot express enough gratitude to Flor Ana, my mentor, editor-of-chief of Indie Earth Publishing, and my friend. You inspire, motivate, and fill my days with such amazing energy for being creative. I forever appreciate Indie Earth for the start of my published works and creative pursuits, and for the learning opportunities and processes they have taken on with me.

Thank you to anyone and everyone, on a range from stranger to close love, for allowing me to be human, be inspired, and follow my dreams through life and all it has to offer. Reader, I wish for you to have such a love for life that anything you grasp feels purely like the person you are and strive to be.

The support that has been given to me from friends, family, and acquaintances has been immense and allows me to value my own efforts, perspectives, and growth. A variety of my poems are truly dedicated to those who make my days warmer.

Finally, to my forever person, my muse, my simplicity: Michael, my deepest love and thanks. You make the sunshine brighter, the days feel cozier, the air feel easier to breath, and my hand and heart serene in your gentle hold. With all of my soul, thank you for the experience and consistent everlasting love in the past, present, and future.

My heartfelt recognition to you all.

About The Author

Kendall Hope is a Colorado native, who thrives off of sunshine and has been a creative since the time she was small. She loves exploring the outdoors and being a part of nature—with the self-recognition that she is nature—which translates to her poetry. Always working towards the next creative step, Kendall finds satisfaction in the little things, which help her stay present. She debuts as an author with her poetry collection, *Pockets of Lavender*.

Visit www.kendallhopepoetry.com to learn more.

Or visit Kendall on Instagram at @kendallhopepoetry

INDIE EARTH

PUBLISHING

About The Publisher

Indie Earth Publishing is an author-first, independent publishing company based in Miami, FL, dedicated to giving artists and writers the creative freedom they deserve in publishing their poetry, fiction, and short stories. We provide our authors a plethora of services that are meant to make them feel like they are finally releasing the book of their dreams, including professional editing, design, formatting, organization, advanced reader teams, and so much more. With Indie Earth Publishing, you're more than just another author, you're part of the Indie Earth creative family, making a difference in the world, one book at a time.

www.indieearthbooks.com

For inquiries, please email:
indieearthpublishinghouse@gmail.com

Instagram: @indieearthbooks

Poetry Prompts for the Reader

Prompt 1:

Pick a poem from each section and write how you feel,
forming your own poem.

Use the next page to write your poem.

Pockets of Lavender

Prompt 2:

Write about how *Pockets of Lavender* influenced your own
mindset and emotions in a poem.

Use the next page to write your poem.

Pockets of Lavender

Prompt 3:

Write a poem to yourself at the age of 27, whether you haven't reached that age, are that age, or have past that age.

Use the next page to write your poem.

Pockets of Lavender

Feel free to share any of your writings and thoughts from these prompts with Kendall:

Instagram: @kendallhopepoetry

Email: kendallhopepoetry@gmail.com

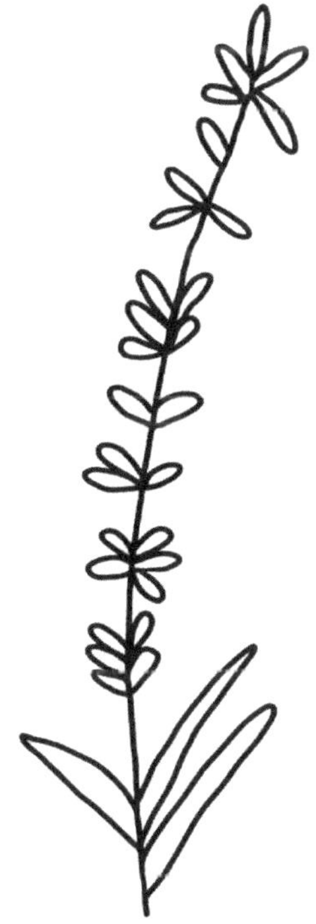